HOW YOU CAN BECOME A BETTER YOU

Eric Frick

Published by Eric Frick 2017.

Updated 07/2019

Copyright © 2017 Eric Frick.

While every precaution has been taken in the preparation of this book, the publisher assumes no responsibility for errors or omissions, or for damages resulting from the use of the information contained herein.

Dedication

This book is dedicated to my Father Roy K. Frick. He was a great inspiration in my life and a role model for everyone who knew and worked with him. Although he passed away in 2008, his influence on his family, students and co-workers will leave a lasting legacy.

Contents

Dedication	5
Contents	7
Foreword	9
1 Persistence	13
2 Find Your Calling	20
3 Learn to Power Through	26
4 Chipping Away	32
5 Take Care of Yourself	38
6 Positive Outlook	45
7 Quiet Time	52
8 Financial Advice	57
9 Keep Your Mind Sharp	64
10 Make a Plan	70
11 Pace Your Work	76
12 Lead By Example	82

13 Build It Yourself	**89**
14 Become You 2.0	**95**
15 Change the World!	**104**
15 Summary	**111**
16 About the Author	**114**

Foreword

Hello and welcome to the book! This book is definitely a new adventure for me since all of my prior publications have been technical materials. Don't worry I won't bore you with theories or equations in this book. I decided to write this book while I was building my online teaching business. I have read a number of books and listened to a number of online videos that have helped me learn the business of building an online business. While wading through all of that material it dawned on me that although this information was helpful, I had a number of life lessons that I have learned over the years that were really my guiding principles that have helped me to begin to build out my life's dream, my own business.

This book is not a self-help or a get rich quick book, so if you are looking for that, you are in the wrong place. It is also not a 30-day plan, crash diet or regimen that you must implement to become a "super" you. It is, however, a number of life lessons that I have learned through several role models in my life that I thought I would pass on to others as they might find them useful in bringing some better peace, tranquility, and productivity to your life.

You may think that a number of these lessons are a bit trite as they may be based on some very simple concepts—but I have found them to be great advice to help simplify things for me and afford me a measure of success in a number of areas in my life.

My criteria for success has definitely changed in my life. Earlier in my career, I was hell-bent on becoming the next multi-billionaire and a major power broker. Now my goals and success criteria are more focused on things that allow for me to have a better night's sleep, a better sense of well-being and things that allow me to have freedom in my life. In general, I look for things that allow me to be me and embrace the best things that life has to offer.

Who am I to offer such advice to you? What qualifies me to dole out such lofty guidance to you that might change your life? My answer to that is I did not invent any of these concepts but rather observed them from others that were role models in my life. I will not name some of these individuals specifically in this book as this may embarrass them as most of these people that I have observed are very private types of people. The major exception to this is my father, Roy K. Frick. Many of the stories and observations in this book are directly from my experiences with him. He passed away on June 2, 2008. He was truly a great man, an inspiration to all who knew him.

For the remainder of this book, I will jump through a number of areas that I have observed and have recorded and some key examples of how my role models either successfully implemented this concept or how they taught me how to implement this in my life. I hope this provides value to you on your life's journey and helps you find some measure of success in whatever ventures that will take you to the top of your mountain.

1 Persistence

"Success is the result of perfection, hard work, learning from failure, loyalty, and persistence."
Colin Powell

I did not organize all of the chapters in this book in a specific order. Most of them were from a quick brainstorming session I had during one of my quiet times (A later chapter in this book). Having said this, the first couple of the chapters in this book have perhaps a deeper inspiration behind them. The very first chapter deals with persistence. I think for most people this lesson will serve them well to help in those difficult times when things seem to be not going your way.

My father had a Ph.D. in Industrial and Systems Engineering from The Ohio State University and became a well-respected tenured professor later in life at the University of Dayton. Although he had very lofty academic and work credentials, he was a very humble man. I remember growing up having a conversation about his Ph.D. and asked him if he thought that people with advanced degrees were really that much smarter than anyone else? He quickly told me that just having an advanced degree, did not make you any smarter than anyone else, but it did indicate that you had a level of perseverance to finish what you started.

Getting a Phd., a medical degree or in fact, any other advanced degree requires you to engage and finish a long and grueling process. In particular, the dissertation process of a Ph.D. requires you to finish an independent research process and then publish and defend those result to an academic committee. Many candidates fail in this part of the process and the independent work that is required presents special challenges along the way.

In my father's case, like most candidates, he also had difficulty along the way. In fact, earlier in his career, he flunked out of graduate school at Ohio State when he was busy working, raising a family and juggling priorities. Through some hard work and dedication, he was able to get academically reinstated and eventually finish his degree.

Several years ago I started my very first online venture of filming and recording an online class. My family thought that I had lost my mind. I built a makeshift video studio in the basement and began recording videos. The first results were remarkably bad. My first videos were very reminiscent of some type of hostage video and or poor quality. However, bit by bit I was able to improve a small amount at a time until I began to achieve some credible results. Now energized by this success I forged ahead to record the rest of my very first video class and published the results.

I published my first class on a platform called Udemy. This is an online website that allows instructors to publish video classes on any number of subjects and either sell them or provide them free of charge. I submitted my class for publishing then after several quality assurances fix it was finally approved and published. So with great anticipation, I waited for the money and sales to come rolling in. Chirping crickets. Nothing.

Wow, I really hit a dead stop. I had no idea how to market my content or even the next step to take. Out of desperation, I decided to change my price from $20 to a free class. Several hours later I got an email that one student signed up, then one more and then another. It turned out that by changing the price I got picked up on a free coupon site and it was a holiday weekend. I had about 1,200 people sign up that weekend. Although I did not make any money from the process, I knew that there was an audience for my material.

Monetizing my content would be a much more difficult step in the process, but relying on some of my persistence I had learned from some of my mentors I was able to slowly, but surely build my online business. Today I have over 13,000 students from 150 countries on Udemy and hope to continue to grow my business further over time. I currently publish my classes under the publisher name of Destin Learning and you can check it out here: Destin Learning on Udemy.

My last example of persistence is from my daughter Alexandra. Alexandra (Alex) was born with Cerebral Palsy and has a number of medical issues. She is only 14 years old and has had well over 20 surgical procedures in her young life. To say that she has had a number of challenges in her life is a vast understatement. No parent is ever prepared to deal with a child with special needs. It just kind of happens and you have to deal with extraordinary circumstances the best that you can. Being a parent of such a child will change your life forever in a number of ways.

Since Alex was born, my family has been a part of a number of events and met a number of people in the special needs community. I'm quite sure I would have never been a part of this community had it not been for Alex. Through the interaction with this community, I have met a number of remarkable people and families. Without exception, all of the people I have met have been truly inspirational. If you have never been a part of this community I encourage you to get involved with one of these organizations. I assure you it will change your life and the lives of others for the better.

So with all of this, you might be wondering what this has to do with persistence? When Alex was a baby and with her diagnosis, we were not sure what mobility Alex would have. One of the clues that she had some major type of medical issues was her difficulty in controlling her motor skills. I will never forget Alex learning how to walk. Ever. I was not sure if she would ever walk, but she, herself, would not give up. Seeing her overcome every obstacle along the way was the definition of persistence.

She still has difficulty with her motor skills and a host of medical issues, but she can walk on her own and shows the same persistence in learning most new things. The picture at the beginning of this chapter is of Alex at a Special Olympics track meet. Alex may take longer to learn things than other people, but she never gives up on anything. She will remain one of my biggest inspirations.

2 Find Your Calling

"Choose a job you love, and you will never have to work a day in your life."
Confucius

In this chapter, I am going to talk about finding your calling. Do you have that sinking feeling in your stomach every Sunday evening about 4:00 in the afternoon? You know the work week is about to approach and you have to revert back into work mode. What if you could escape that feeling and truly love the work that you do? No more Mondays. No more sinking feeling. Imagine the productivity you could achieve if you were working on something you truly loved to do.

I am sure you have met people who have actually found their calling. You can tell by talking to them for just a few minutes. They love to talk about what they do and really seem to have a true peace about them. These types of people are truly comfortable in their own skin and have a real sense of pride in their work. Having a job that pays great and has great perks really will not do it for you if you are miserable in the work that you do.

Several years ago I had an opportunity to interview for a part-time teaching job at a local university. As the interview got closer, I was making excuses in my mind not to go and blow it off. The interview was in front of a faculty panel and all the other applicants as well. The format was to give a presentation on the class that you were interested in teaching.

The only problem was you were not allowed to use PowerPoint for the presentation, you could use anything else instead. I was really nervous and was thinking about canceling out, but my wife Amy kicked me in the pants and made me go and get it done. She is a great motivator in that way. Anyhow, I went and it went really well. Several weeks later I was teaching my first class and beginning to find that this work was something I really enjoyed. I have since then taught many classes, formed my own online teaching business and written several books. I have found my calling, but I almost walked away from it. I have my wife Amy to thank for that. I am still working on ways to teach more and work less on my day job, but at least at this time, I am not trying to sort out in my mind what I really want to do.

Another person I know who has found their calling is my mother-in-law, Diane. She works in the organ and tissue business. A number of years ago she went back to school to complete her undergraduate and a graduate degree. She did this while working, traveling all over the US and abroad. After she had completed both degrees, the college she attended asked her to be in a television commercial to talk about her work and how she was able to utilize what she learned in school on the job. Once I viewed the commercial, it was easy to tell the pride she had in her work and how important it was to her that her business helped save people's lives and really made a difference in the world. She views her work as far more than a job and it shows in how she approaches her daily routine.

My church pastor, Tim, is another great example of someone I know who have found their calling. Most pastors are passionate people who can really rally the congregation with their weekly sermons, but with Pastor Tim, you can tell that there is no other job in the world that he would rather be doing. In fact, I remember in one of his sermons, he stated that he felt that this was the specific job and the specific church he was meant to be working in. The congregation at our church really appreciates the level of commitment he has for our congregation. When you talk to him it is easy to sense his great enthusiasm for his work.

If you have not found your calling, how do you find it? If I had a magic formula for that I would share it with you and make it happen. I do know that if you don't like what you are doing you need to work on changing things up in your life. I'm not telling you to quit your job and move to Vegas, but looking to move into new things and grow yourself as a person will pay great dividends in your life. If you have some things in the back of your mind that you have always wanted to pursue or try, maybe now is the time to move ahead with some of those ideas?

I think if you can be creative with your thinking you can try some things out without breaking the bank. Maybe these things are not a new full-time job, but more like pursuing a new hobby like painting or writing a book. Many times you can invest some of your time in these things and not sink a large amount of money in order to get started. Once you try something it may not be what you thought it would be. You can only find out by digging a bit deeper. Try and find the things you really love doing and give it a try. Make sure it is something you dream about and not something that someone else is talking you into. Living someone else's dream may not be that great of a deal for you.

I hope that something in this chapter has inspired you to think about your calling in life and how you might find it. If you by some chance have already found your calling I am truly glad for you. Maybe you can help someone else down that path? In any case, good luck in fulfilling your dream.

3 Learn to Power Through

"There is nothing happens to any person but what was in his power to go through with."
Marcus Aurelius

I think it is fitting that I am writing this chapter while I am sitting in my daughter's hospital room. She has been in and out of the hospital over the last few years with a host of medical issues. Although Nationwide Children's Hospital is a terrific facility, it is a very draining process to stay here for an extended period of time. My wife Amy has taken most of the shifts here. I have never met anyone who has more stamina and patience than she has. She is an incredible woman. She seems to have the innate ability to "Power Through" where I really have to work at it.

My first introduction to this concept "Power Through" came to me while I was working as a Software Development Manager at a startup company. This company was building a robotic system for dispensing medication. This robot was designed to be a large-scale system for pharmacies that were dispensing large amounts of medication to nursing homes. It had that capacity to serve as many as 10,000 patients per day and could be loaded with 1,400 different types of medication. This was a complex piece of hardware and software. Accuracy was extremely important.

The initial software development effort for this project had gone horribly wrong. I was hired to right the ship on the software side and get things moving. I ended up firing the entire development team and starting a new team to finish the job. Because of the initial problems with the software development, the project was delayed six months.

Even though the project was delayed six months, there was still an impossible amount of work to do. Any logical way of laying out the schedule never added up to get the product out the door in any reasonable timeframe. As the deadline came closer we moved the project team on site where the first robot was going into production in Baltimore MD. Both the software team and the engineering team relocated from our home base in Columbus, OH to Baltimore to shorten the development cycle.

As the team began to ramp up we began to make rapid progress. We were working ridiculous hours from 8 am in the morning until 10 or 11 pm in the evening. We also began to work weekends as well, in order to cram every last working hours into the project before going live. This schedule went on for about eight weeks until we finally went live into production.

I will never forget during one of our really difficult stretches in that phase of the project, our CEO, Rick D'Angelo, gave a short speech to fire up the team. He explained that most startup companies fail because that can't "Power Through." They get close to delivering a product, but can't push the ball over the goal line. He went on to explain that this was our time to really press to make this happen. I'm not sure the speech was the only thing that motivated the team, but the team did share a sense of purpose for getting this project done.

In this case, the team was able to power through and successfully launch the product. When you are part of something like this you realize it is more than just the number of hours you put in or following a well-scripted plan, it is a mindset that the team develops that allows them to succeed despite many obstacles.

Several years later I had shifted gears a bit in my career and was interested in pursuing a teaching career. After teaching part-time in the evenings for several years, I had the dream of developing my own online business. This was to sell courses and books on software development over the Internet. While this may sound like a simple process, I assure you that learning to film and edit video while producing a credible result requires a lot of work. I had gotten to a point where I had published my first course and offered it free to get an initial following of students. This class was well received and I was now in a position to follow up with my first paying class. I struggled to get it out the door. It seemed that everything in the universe was conspiring against me so that I could not complete this.

At this point, I was wondering if my newfound dream was a bust. At some point, I remembered my experiences with the robot and how to "Power Through." A series of late night sessions and a few weekends finished the job. I still am not sure my classes will make me rich, but as of today I have produced five online classes and published three books and counting. I currently have over 13,000 students from 150 countries with more on the way. I had really reached a stalled point but found a way to break past that obstacle.

I think everyone has various projects that are close to completion, but you are having trouble finishing. Many times these projects weigh heavily on your mind. Most of these times you just need one final push to get to completion. You just need to learn to Power Through! Final results are so rewarding!

4 Chipping Away

"The three great essentials to achieve anything worthwhile are, first, hard work, second, stick-to-itivness; third, common sense."
Thomas A Edison

In this chapter, I am going to talk about chipping away at a large project to really accomplish a long-term goal. Once again I am writing from my daughter's hospital room. If you are noticing a theme you are correct. It's Sunday evening and I am tired from a long weekend and from sleeping limited hours and a few nights here in the hospital. I'm not complaining, but am using this to illustrate my point. I have set a goal for myself to author a large amount of content before the end of this year. If I look at the entire body of work it will become easy to become overwhelmed. I have set a long-term goal to grow my online education business with the dream of working at it full time.

At the time of this writing, my business is still very small, but it is starting to grow steadily as I produce more material. My major project for this year is to produce a programmer boot camp that will show beginners how to program in Microsoft .NET. The class will result in my authoring a series of 10 books this year as well as several hundred videos. Since I have over 25 years of experience as a software developer and manager I am very familiar with the content. I have also taught this content at the university level as well. My major problem is I am new to the world of delivering content online and this is my first venture into self-publishing. If you break all of this down, it almost seems insurmountable at times.

The one concept I have learned over the years to combat this feeling is the concept of "chipping away." If you take a really large task and break it down into component parts, then maybe knocking one task after the other is not such a big deal. Just put your head down and start doing instead of thinking. One of the things I like to do is have a clear visualization of short-term tasks. That way I can see what I need to do. I have a really big whiteboard in my office at home and one of the things I put up on the board is my checklist of things to do. Many people have commented on this and ask why I don't do this in some type of high tech way on an app or on the web? I like the visibility of the whiteboard. It is in my face and helps me motivate to check one item off the list after the other. I try to have a really short-term focus for this list so I can focus on the tasks at hand. I have spreadsheets and other nerd stuff for long-term planning, but I depend on the whiteboard to motivate me day by day.

My very first experience with this concept is when I built out a room at home in our unfinished basement. I suppose this kind of project is some type of Dad's right of passage. I really needed the space and had to get this done for the home of my future online business. Like most newbies, I went into planning overdrive. I drew plans, thought up new ideas, and obsessed over the project in only the way an engineer can do. I had done months of planning and still no office in the basement. Out of desperation I even hired a contractor to build the entire thing. Luckily, I was able to get out of the contract when I realized I could not afford it. The project was way out of my initial scope.

I was really discouraged at this point. During this time I remember a phone conversation I had with my Dad. I complained that I really did not have any building experience and did not think I could pull this off. He encouraged me and reminded me he had completed a job like this on his own and told me that if he could do it so could I. He also told me to quit over planning this and just get started. Do a little bit at a time. Later that day I went out and bought some lumber and started framing my first wall. Over the next few months, I chipped away at the basement and did a little bit at a time until I had a complete TV room and office. The construction is by no means perfect, but I learned a great deal in doing this project. I have a home office for my side business now for many years.

Large projects can overwhelm us. Whether they are projects at work or projects at home, some of these large-scale efforts can really cause us to freeze up. I'm sure many of you are laughing at the idea that building a simple room in the basement is a large project, but from my perspective, at that time, it was enough to slow me down to the point that I could not move forward. I'm sure most people will tell you that getting started on a project is the hardest and extremely difficult, but continuing on it has its challenges as well. Coming up with a plan and a method to keep cranking away on a project will allow you to take on truly life-changing projects. I can't say with certainty that my online teaching business will be an overwhelming financial success, or will allow me the freedom to work without a regular day job, but I will tell you that I will chip away to complete my ten-book .NET developer series.

I hope that if you find yourself in a rut you will think about how to chip away at that project, or at that long-term goal that is in your mind as a dream. Now that I have finished this chapter, I can now cross off the last checklist item I had on my whiteboard at home once I get back from the hospital. Good luck in your efforts at chipping away.

5 Take Care of Yourself

"And now that you don't have to be perfect, you can be good."
John Steinbeck

Taking care of yourself both physically and mentally determines to a large extent the energy and vitality you have and your ability to take on large and complex projects and complete them. If you are constantly physically and mentally drained, it will be difficult if not impossible for you to perform your best on the task at hand.

Once again, I will note a disclaimer here that I am not by any stretch of the imagination, any type of fitness guru. I have a problem like many people keeping my weight under control and getting regular exercise. I have found a couple of things that really help me in the long term staying focused. One of the things I think of in this area is the analogy of the standard speech that flight attendants make before a flight about the oxygen mask. Put your mask on first if you are traveling with small children so you can help them. I think of taking care or yourself in much the same way, if you are not taking good care of yourself it will be difficult for you to help others.

The one thing I have found for sure is that exercise is really necessary during times of high stress. When I have been working on really stressful projects, I find getting even a little bit of regular exercise helps. Even if it is as simple as a short walk, and just getting some light exercise really lets your mind relax and give you some time to recharge. Your diet can play a key part as well, but if you travel for work this can be especially difficult. I have traveled off and on for work for a number of years and you can probably plot my major weight gains against my travel time. If you can manage to make some time for exercise during travel, it can really help with the food binges as well.

One key I have found for exercise is to find something you really enjoy. I tried for years to get into a routine of running and tried to get that going. I tried going to the track starting short distances and then working up a little at a time. Nothing really worked. I am pretty sure I failed because I really hated to run. Later I started using a rowing machine and for some reason I really enjoyed it. Since I really liked to row, I was able to continue and become more regular with going to the gym. Don't get me wrong, I still struggle to keep a regular routine, but rowing has been my most successful attempt. For a while, one of the people I worked with was also rowing and we found a way to compete online. That little bit of competition really moved both of us forward for a time. We have both moved on to other jobs, but even now and then I will still text him "1500 meters today." If you can find someone to help motivate you it really helps. I have a semi-regular basketball game with my son a couple of times a week. He is six foot three inches tall and I am five foot eight so you can guess the outcome.

Maybe another trick in the bag to get some exercise is doing some outdoor work. I know my dad hated yard work and work around the house. I must admit that I'm not a huge fan of cutting the grass, but I do like to get out to wash and wax the car. I find that cleaning up the car while blasting some music is a great time for me to unwind out in the sunshine. Maybe you can find some of those tasks that will let you unwind outside, exercise, all while getting some fresh air?

The picture at the beginning of this chapter is of my daughter Alexandra skiing a few years ago. Alexandra (we call her Alex) has Cerebral Palsy and has difficulty with her motor skills. At the time when she went skiing, I was not sure she could do this at all. They had some special equipment that could help her out and they had some people trained to help with adaptive skiing. They had her skiing down the hill in no time. I have since learned not to try and guess what Alex can and can't do. She always amazes me.

As part of the adaptive ski program, they offered to have the parents ski as well. It had been several years since I had been skiing and I was about to just skip since I was not sure I could still ski without hurting myself. The day we went to the slopes was a day devoted to having the entire ski area dedicated to an adaptive ski day. I had never really seen skiing like that before. To see how many people overcome their difficulties and learn to ski with special equipment was truly amazing.

After seeing that, I got up on the slopes with my daughter and had a great time. My excuse for not skiing was because I was a bit older and out of shape seemed pretty lame after seeing the amazing skill and devotion all of the other skiers were showing that day. I also remember watching some Warren Miller ski movies years before. If you have not watched any of these movies you really need to before you go on a ski trip. They will really pump you up before you go. Anyway, I remember one of his famous quotes talking about skiing, "if you don't do it this year, you will be one year older when you do." I think you can apply this to just about anything.

So I hope that you can find some creative way to take care of yourself. I think taking care of yourself is much more than just forcing yourself to go to the gym or starting a crash diet. Maybe it is more of a mindset to find some things that you enjoy doing that are also good for you physically and mentally. If you are finding that you are torturing yourself with an exercise routine you hate, maybe you can adjust and find something you have much-increased odds or repeating on a regular basis. Ok after this I am going to go and row. I promise.

6 Positive Outlook

"A positive attitude causes a chain reaction of positive thoughts, events, and outcomes. It is a catalyst and it sparks extraordinary results."
Wade Boggs

In this chapter, I am going to talk about the importance of having a positive attitude. I will tell you right now that on some days this is really hard to do. Sometimes things have a way of ganging up on you. I can't tell you how many bad days that I have had where it was just unbelievable that all of the bad or upsetting events piled up on the same day. If I look back on most of these events they don't seem nearly as upsetting as they were at the time. On these types of days, it is easy to take your frustrations out on whoever happens to be near you at the time. Usually the next day you look back on that as being a mistake.

Having a bad day and getting through it is one thing, but truly developing a positive attitude is quite another. I have worked in the software and IT business for my entire career. I have worked on developing and supporting many large mission-critical systems. During this work, I have been a part of many difficult problem situations. In some cases, I was the responsible individual for really large systems with a lot of money at stake. On many occasions, I had to go into my boss's office and deliver bad news. That is never a fun thing to do. Whenever I have faced these situations I have tried to be the person in the room that focuses on solving the situation in a positive way. Many times, in these difficult situations, everyone's first reaction is to play the blame game and let some steam off. This is OK to a point, but as a group, you have to move on quickly to developing a solution to the problem. It really helps in these situations to try and take the emotion out of the situation and just move on. Again this is not as simple as it sounds, but sometimes you just have to take the verbal beating, defuse the situation and move on. Being as positive as you can will help defuse the situation more quickly.

Being a positive person can really help with group dynamics. I have been part of a large number of group projects both in school and work environments. Once a group starts to go negative, it is hard to keep any type of positive focus. While working on a project abroad I was part of an onsite engineering team that lived and worked together for an extended period of time. After the team was together for a few months we all began to miss home. The group then began to complain about our current environment. The complaining got worse and worse to the point that I was miserable as well as everyone else. I too missed home but realized the group was beginning to develop its own negative dynamic. Unfortunately, at that point, there was not much to do about it and the contract was soon to be over. My point is, you may encounter this situation and if you realize you are being pulled by the group, you might have the ability to influence the group dynamic to be in a better frame of mind. Working with a group of miserable people is a draining experience. Looking back on it, we really had nothing to complain about, but we allowed the group to fall into a deep rut. If you find yourself in this situation you can look at ways to influence a positive environment or maybe begin to distance yourself from the group to improve your own peace of mind.

I have worked in a number of organizations over the years and since much of my career has been as a contractor, I have been able to see a large number of customer environments as well. Having observed many work environments, one of the things you quickly pick up on are the personalities that everyone has difficulty working with. You also quickly find those staff members who are the go-to people in those organizations. In almost every case those go to people were the ones with the most positive attitudes in the company. No one likes to work with someone who is always negative. In fact, many times people will do almost anything to avoid them. If you can develop that truly positive attitude you will find that you may become one of these go to people in your workplace. I'm not talking about being the company cheerleader here, but being someone who really wants to help people and make a positive difference in their environment.

How you take care of yourself can have a huge impact on your attitude and outlook. If you are tired and hungover at work you most probably will not be at your best. When you are sick or not feeling well, you will not treat people as well as you would on a normal day. In some situations, you will not have the luxury of calling off sick but will need to make the best of those situations. I'm not sure I have a magic bullet cure for this situation, but I do think it is helpful to explain to the people around you that you might not be at your best.

Being as positive as you can, will help you handle many difficult situations that life can throw at you. Many times as things work out we may be dealing with difficult situations at work and at home simultaneously. If you have a real crisis situation with your family and you have a high-stress job at the same time, it will require just about everything you have in your bag of tricks to remain positive. I'm sure that many of these family crisis situations you will not want to share with your work associates, but it will help to mention that there are some things going on that might have you a bit distracted. People that work with you closely every day will notice a change in your demeanor and it is usually better to just admit that something is going on that is bothering you. That does not mean you have to share the details with them, but if you are in a leadership position it is probably best to warn everyone you might not be the same person that they usually are dealing with.

I have found over time that having some activities that can clear your mind will help greatly in developing a positive attitude. Having a regularly scheduled time to exercise and having some time that you can mentally escape from the daily grind can help you emotionally reload for the long work day. Also finding opportunities to see and share some humor in your daily routine will help you find a much better balance in your life. Being positive will pay many benefits for you in your career, in your family life, in your health, and in your personal well being. It will not be easy to always be positive, but you may find yourself sleeping better at night if you can shift that positive balance in your mind.

7 Quiet Time

"Some of the most powerful times are when we're quiet."
Michael W. Smith

The modern world is filled with all kinds of distractions. These distractions are more than just the cell phone, Twitter, constant texts and other continuous noise that comes at us throughout the day. They represent a continuous flow where we are simply reacting to the flood of things that are coming at us in a non-stop barrage. All of us need a time where we can step away for a few minutes every day and truly reflect on what is important in our lives.

My inspiration for this advice comes from a sermon from my church pastor. I'm sure pastor Tim thought I was in a deep slumber the morning he talked about quiet time and it's importance in our lives. Most of the words he speaks resonate with me, but this message, in particular, seemed to really hit home with me.

I have worked in the IT business for my entire my professional career. In particular, I have worked in software development and IT operations. For most of my career, it has not been uncommon for my phone to ring at all hours of the day or night. In addition, most workdays are filled with interruptions, problems that need immediate attention and meetings that can't wait. After days and long stretches like these, I frequently require a dose of quiet time to recharge my batteries. I don't care how hardened a road warrior you are downtime is necessary to keep you on an even keel.

For me, I try to have a short quiet time every morning before I start my day. It is not always easy, but I generally have about 10 minutes before my daughter gets on the bus. No cell phone, no email, no head banging music. A cup of coffee and the dog hanging out at my feet to keep me company. It is tempting to use this time to do one last email check or check the voicemail from the day before. I find a short recharge with a bit of reflection really sets a good tone for the day. Your quiet time may not look exactly like this, but I think you will know when are in recharge mode and how to use that time to quiet your nerves and get a bit of renewal time.

In addition to a short time of recharge every day, sometimes a really deep recharge is necessary. The answer is extended quiet time! The picture at the front of this chapter is from the deck of my parent's townhouse in Destin, Florida. My mother and father have been gracious over the years and have allowed my family to vacation here numerous times. I try to get down twice a year and use the time to hang out at the beach and get some extended downtime. The sunsets in Destin, Florida are incredibly beautiful. The picture I included does not do it justice at all. The hours I have spent on the deck have helped me find my place to unwind all of the stress that I have built up since my last visit. Your place to recharge may not be the beach, it may even be in your own backyard, but finding a place like this that you can visit on a regular basis will pay lifetime dividends.

I'm not sure how this got started, but every time I now go to Destin I text my buddies in Ohio to let them know I am back in Destin. They have visited me down there several times and they have seen first hand the incredible scenery from the deck and also the recharging power of the quiet time at the beach. I'll close with the contents of my semi-annual text to them. I wish you great success with your own version of quiet time.

Happy spring boys it's been a long hard winter!

8 Financial Advice

"I can understand wanting to have millions of dollars, there's a certain freedom, meaningful freedom, that comes with that. But once you get much beyond that, I have to tell you, it's the same hamburger."
Bill Gates

In this chapter, I will talk about some basic financial advice. I will warn you right up front that I am not a financial guru and I don't have a magic method for making you rich quick. I have made decent money for most of my career and have made plenty of mistakes that I have learned from. I have also observed some of my close friends and family that have been financially successful and will pass those lessons along in this chapter.

My first and foremost recommendation to you is to avoid debt as much as possible in your life. It is something that can quickly spiral out of control and really ruin your life. For various reasons, I have carried a heavy debt load for most of my life. I will tell you it takes a toll on you to continue to run on the treadmill to continue paying the bills. If you can pay cash for things as much as possible. Running up big bills usually starts with one simple purchase and then another followed by yet another. The interest rates begin. Soon you are arranging a complex schedule just to make ends meet. It then begins to spiral out of control from there. There are a variety of really good programs out there to help you manage this and I will recommend my favorite in a bit.

The one tried and true method for making a lot of money is to make regular investments over a very long period of time. This method requires a great deal of discipline to make it work. Setting up some type of payroll deduction to put money aside from every paycheck is probably one of the best methods available. Invest the money before you even see it. Start small and then scale up from there. Many people complain if they only start at $50 or $100 at a time it is too little. You will be amazed at how regular investments will grow if you continue to invest small amounts over a long period of time. Again, chip away at this.

Another great way to build wealth long term is to build equity in real estate. For many people who have not saved any money over their lifetimes, this may be their only asset. Unless you live in a really high demand area you will probably not see a spectacular return for your investment in your home, but over the long term, even modest appreciation will help you build your net worth substantially.

If you can branch out over time and own multiple properties it might make the case even better. My mother and father scraped together enough money early in my father's career to buy an investment property in Destin, Florida. Some of the photos you have seen in this book are from that back deck. Although it was difficult for them in the early days to make payments on two properties, over time the beach property appreciated substantially. Today it represents a key asset in my mother's retirement investment portfolio. Also, she is kind enough to allow my family to vacation there as well. Thanks, Mom!

The best method for all of these methods is to start as early as possible. Long-term investing really works its magic if interest is compounded over as long of a term as possible. The problem with this is you generally make the least amount of money early in your career and really need most of your income just to survive. I will tell you from experience, cut back on the beer money and throw some in the bank it will be worth it later. Even if you did not get started early do not use that as an excuse to not get started at all. It is never too late to start saving and investing.

My last piece of advice is to find a trusted advisor to help you lay out your financial plans. This may not be easy since there are tons of frauds out there trying to scam you out of your money. The best place to start is if there is someone in your immediate family you can ask for advice or perhaps they can recommend someone to use for financial planning and advice. I would also recommend Dave Ramsey who I have followed over the last few years. He offers a program called Financial Peace University that I have taken and highly recommend. His methods and plans are very conservative and effective. You can Google his name and find him online.

I'm sure you have heard much of this advice somewhere before, but these are time-tested principles. I have seen them work in dramatic ways in my immediate family. Hopefully, if I stay the course I will become financially independent over the next few years as well. Patience and persistence will help you with your goals in this area of your life.

In my closing notes, please remember that your net worth does not define you as a person. Having a lot of money does not necessarily make you some type of great individual, it only means you have more money in your bank account. Sometimes it is difficult for us to keep this in perspective. Please treat this in your life for what it is. We all want the have nice things for ourselves and our family, but obsessing over these things is not worth the pain and anguish it will cause you in your mind. Make and invest money like you are playing a video game. If you find yourself good at it great if you don't then find another game. I hope you have the best of luck in all of your financial dealings. Good luck!

9 Keep Your Mind Sharp

"An investment in knowledge pays the best interest."
Benjamin Franklin

I have worked in the software development business for almost thirty years. It sounds scary when I actually write those numbers down. Anyway, the software development business changes rapidly. New techniques and languages are introduced at a rapid rate. I have taught many aspiring programmers through my online teaching and in the university environment as well. The students first thought is to learn a programming language and master it. One of the things I always caution students about is that these languages change rapidly and as soon as you learn one another one will take its place. To become a successful programmer you really need to embrace a program of lifelong learning about software development and this needs to take place outside your nine to five job. The really great programmers are always learning and continuously adapting to change. They attend seminars, read blogs, watch videos and keep up with the numerous trade journals.

When I started teaching, the entire learning experience changed for me in a very positive way. I often heard other teachers say that you really don't learn something until you teach it to someone else. That rang very true for me once I was faced with the task of teaching someone else many of the things I had worked on for my entire career. I'm not sure I understood the material any better but may have picked up on some of the smaller nuances that you need to understand to give a really good explanation to someone else. When you are teaching a room full of people they are liable to ask just about any question you can imagine. Those questions often will help you understand the material on a much deeper level. If you don't know it all the first time in a class, you will be the second time through. The surprising thing about the process is how the students will actually help the instructor learn the material better.

Learning is also not an age driven thing. Sometimes I have seen people later in life learn interesting new skills and continue their journey of lifelong learning. When my father retired, I think my family expected him to continue doing some highly technical engineering work since that is what he did for his entire career. At some point soon after he retired, he told me and my sisters that he was taking up painting. I think we all laughed and thought he was joking, but he was quite serious and told us about some classes he had signed up for. Looking back, I think my family thought he would take one class and then move on to something else. To our surprise, he really got into it and started to produce some really good drawings. His work got better and better and he moved on from drawings to paintings. When my wife and I bought our new house he surprised us with a Christmas gift of a painting of our new home. That painting still hangs in my living room today and is one of my prized possessions.

When I started my online business, to say I faced a learning challenge, was an understatement. I started with teaching video classes online and had to learn basic filmmaking skills. Learning to shoot a decent video in my basement was a challenging process. Sound, lighting, scripts and decent editing are all essential to making a credible educational video. My early results were not very good, but I kept finding more and more material to study and improved the process.

After I got to a certain point of improving the process and learning the new techniques it became fun. I think with many new tasks the beginning steps are much more painful than after you get going a bit. The problem for many of these things is getting over the hump so you can begin to enjoy the fruits of your labor. A few small successes are really motivating.

As I got deeper into my online business, I began working with my son. At first, he just wanted an easy summer job and I was happy to help. After he was working with me for a while, we began to try some other things to try and expand the business. Some of this was working with online sales and marketing. This was really new for both of us and we learned those things together. Learning as part of a team or a group can also help motivate you to learn new things in new and interesting ways. We are still working on expanding our business and learning new things together and having fun with the process. This is the power of brainstorming.

If you are like me I can get really deep into solving problems you are working on. Sometimes I find I need to put things down and relax for a while. If I get too involved with fixing a problem or if I get stuck on something, I need to decompress. Other times I also find that I might need to change things up for a while to keep things fresh. If I am learning something new I try to rotate a couple of different topics so I do not get too much of one of them at a time.

I hope that you are able to find some new things in your life that will keep your mind challenged and you can enjoy a great sense of accomplishment wherever your life takes you. Good luck in keeping your mind sharp.

10 Make a Plan

"In preparing for battle I have always found that plans are useless, but planning is indispensable."
Dwight D. Eisenhower

When I was growing up I always remember that my Dad had a "to do" list that he kept folded up and put in his front shirt pocket. If my sisters read this book, I'm sure this comment will bring a big smile to their faces. I remember thinking that there was no way that when I get older that I would ever do something as nerdy as this. So my method now is to keep my daily list in my back pants pocket. Way cooler! It's funny how we turn into our parents years later even though we swear that we will not.

My daily "to do" list is just a way to remind me of things that fit into a bigger plan for me. I like to work on a plan for my finances and for my work as well. Since I have been working on starting my own business I have been very deep into planning and trying new things. Publishing and selling digital products such as video classes and ebooks is a really new thing for me and planning through this has helped me keep my project on track. It important to have a plan, but you must be able to adjust the plan as things change along the way. This is a delicate balance to know when to keep pressing on the original plan and when to adjust. The only way you can get better at this is to begin the planning and tracking process.

Your plan does not have to be complicated, but it should contain enough detail to help you move into action. I have met many people who love to plan and tinker with plans and then never actually do anything. You can get to a point where you are paralyzed by your plan because of a staggering amount of detail. Getting to the point can be really frustrating. At that point, you really need to take a break and dumb down the plan into something actionable. One step at a time enables you to move forward.

When my father was nearing retirement he was having some difficulties in working out exactly how and when he was going to fully retire. He had invested in some rental property in Florida and also had some short-term debt he was trying to pay off before he fully retired. He talked to me about it and we brainstormed some ideas. He turned those ideas into some simple spreadsheets and we reviewed them together. After he talked through these ideas, it became clear what was the best solution to the problem. When you put something down on paper to explain to someone else, it can really clear things up in your own mind. It also helps to have someone you can talk over ideas with. My Dad and I had a great relationship but I am not sure many parents would share their finances with their children in such detail. It was a good situation for both of us, my father got some additional ideas from me, and I learned how to make some plans of my own from his examples. When my father passed away I was able to help my mother get going again quickly since I was very familiar with my father's financial plan and he was also very organized.

When you are working on your plans try and keep your short-term goals to be achievable, but keep your long-term goals as something you will have to stretch to meet. If your short-term goals are consistently not obtainable you might get frustrated and abandon the process. When you begin this process it just needs to become a part of your routine. For me, every Saturday morning I have some coffee and update the numbers on my financial plan. Sometimes I don't like the numbers I am seeing, but I have a long-term plan that maps out the goals of where I want to be and I keep pressing forward to those goals. In addition, I am folding in the results of more income from my online business as it grows. My stretch goal is to work full time in my online business.

I don't think a plan has to be complicated to be effective. It can be as simple as jotting down some ideas into a notebook over your morning coffee and mapping out how you can act on those ideas. Don't underestimate the power of your mind and how turning your ideas into action can have some amazing results. If you can act on ideas over a really long-term over a number of years you can achieve really remarkable results. Having a well thought out plan can help map out those great ideas in your head into a way to ultimately make those ideas a reality. I hope that the ideas in this chapter have given you the inspiration to help you in your own personal planning process.

11 Pace Your Work

"Nothing will work unless you do"
Maya Angelou

So in earlier chapters, I talked out chipping way and powering through projects. There is a time and place for both of these. Sometimes when a project is near the goal line you need to press a little harder to get it done and finish things off. Other times you need to establish a pace that will not burn the team out and you can have a sustained long period of consistent results.

Pictured above is my son who was much smaller at the time when he helped me out during my basement finishing project. Much of this construction work for me was new at the time. I had done some basic framing work before, but the drywall work and finishing work was new to me. One thing became obvious to me once I started the project as I needed to schedule some regular times to work on this so the project did not stretch out forever. I then scheduled regular hours in the evenings and on the weekends to work on the project in chunks of work at a time. I broke tasks out in phases for the framing, ceiling, drywall etc. Scheduling projects like this were routine for me at work, but it was very different doing this as a home project with just me working on it.

If you can schedule tasks and keep to the schedule you can then take on much larger projects. For me, I now have scheduled a time where I will go to the library to work on my book projects or my online videos. Once I get to the library I will dedicate an hour or whatever time I scheduled and just knock out what I have scheduled to do. The good thing for me about going to the library is there is not much else to do there but just get my work done. I don't wander through the magazine section or check out the exhibits, I just go there to crank out some work. Ok maybe sometimes I get a cup of coffee, but you get the idea.

If you can make a habit of certain things you can change your life in a positive way. Making a time to go to the gym or working on a project in the evening after the rest of your family goes to bed or getting up early every morning to get something done in small chunks of time over a long period can have dramatic results.

Many years ago before I got married I spent a lot of time playing golf. After I graduated from college I joined a golf club and started to play regularly. When I started I was an average golfer, but not very consistent. At some point, I got a bunch of competition from one of my regular playing partners. I decided I really wanted to improve in a big way. At that time I was about a 15 handicap. I signed up for a series of lessons with our club pro who helped me really relearn the golf swing. One of the things he told me was the big ways to improve was to really learn a better way to practice. He taught me how to structure my practice sessions and concentrate on different skills during each session. He also told me that the best players practiced like they were getting paid by the hour. After a while, I really worked hard on my game and eventually brought my handicap down to a 5. I had really improved quite a bit, but most of it was through my improved practice sessions and how I was able to take my practice skill to the course. In addition, I had regularly scheduled practice sessions that I would set up so that I would be ready to go before my next round or club event. That schedule and the structure of these sessions accounted for my major improvements. I don't play nearly as much today due to time commitments and my game is pretty shaky, but I feel pretty confident that if I started back up I could improve back to the point I was before if I utilize those same practice techniques.

So whether your goal is to write a book, improve your golf game, start your own business or something else you can improve your chances of success by pacing your work in the right way. Most long-term results require a major time commitment and those commitments are easier to make if you schedule them in the right way. Take into account your natural tendencies. If you are a morning person it probably won't work well for you to schedule your tasks late at night. Also if you are a night owl you probably won't do well with five AM tasks. Be realistic and make a schedule you can stick to. You might have to get creative and maybe skip your lunch hour and go to the local library to get some things done during the day. So whatever your goal is, start from the top and determine the amount of time you need to put into the task and then try to find the time for those tasks on a regular basis. It's not as easy as it sounds, particularly if you have a family and kids to drive around town. I hope this chapter has given you some ideas and inspiration to pace your work so you can accomplish the project of your dreams. Good luck!

12 Lead By Example

"Setting an example is not the main means of influencing others, it is the only means"
Albert Einstein

Today's world is dominated by news, press releases, the Internet, social media and people giving opinions non-stop 24 hours a day. While all of this communication is good there tends to be a lot of people who are talking and not doing anything. All talk and no action. While voicing your opinion is an important part of a free society, simply talking about something and not backing it up with any action will result in limited credibility. A much more powerful message can be delivered to people around you by leading by example. Several people in my life have illustrated this in simple yet powerful ways. I will outline some of those experiences for you.

The picture at the beginning of this chapter is of my father along with my mother while he was getting his PhD. from The Ohio State University in Industrial and System Engineering. Getting this degree required him to take a year off from work and required our family to move from our house into a small apartment. As anyone who has gone back to school after working knows, this is a very difficult task, particularly when you have a family with small children. I faced a similar challenge when I decided to go back to school to get a Master's degree. I had reached a point where I could get a fairly significant promotion, but it meant that I would not be able to finish my degree. Both my father and my boss at the time advised me against that decision and that the degree would help me more in the long run. I was not sure and debated my decision, but the example that my father had shown me through his sacrifices earlier in my life solidified my decision. As it turned out that decision paid big dividends later in my career as it opened the door for me to begin my teaching career. It turned out to be one of my true joys in life and allowed me to find my calling. I am truly grateful to my former boss and my father for such wise advice. I encourage you to seek out role models that can help you with these types of difficult decisions that you will face in your life.

As it turns out this was not the first or last time my father would teach me some of these life lessons through his actions. While I was growing up my family was very active in the Lutheran church and we went every Sunday to both Sunday school and church. In addition, I spent some extra time there while working on a Boy Scout project. This section of the book is not meant to paint me as some type of saint because I assure you I am not, but it did give me the opportunity to see some of the inner workings of the church. I was surprised by how political the church inner workings were and how many difficulties they had in running the daily operations. People really loved to complain, but did not really pitch in to help. During this time my father did pitch in and become a member of the church council. Rather than just joining in to complain, he took action to dig in and help make things better. He brought some of his professional expertise as an engineer and a manager to help smooth out the operations of the church and make everyone's life just a bit easier.

I also see examples of this in my own household almost every day. My wife Amy is a great example of someone who will pitch in and help at a moments notice. Our daughter Alexandra is involved with one of our local Special Olympics team and Amy is always there to offer her help with fundraising and tasks of all sorts. This may not seem extraordinary, but if you consider she is already the mother of a special needs child that takes considerable extra care her efforts here are truly remarkable. I have seen her on many occasions working on a fundraising spreadsheet while spending the evening in my daughter's hospital room. I don't think you will find that level of commitment in many people you meet.

I also know that Amy learned many of these special talents from her mother Diane. Diane has had an amazing career in the tissue bank industry. She has worked herself from a very humble beginning to being the Chief Operating Officer at one of the largest tissue banks in the country. She has received multiple awards and was elected president of the American Association of Tissue Banks in 2009. She was also able to obtain a bachelors and masters degree while working full time. She did all of this while raising a family. If you ever have the pleasure of meeting her you will see right away she is someone who leads by example. She is someone who walks the walk daily in her life and prefers to show by doing and leading.

I try to use these examples in my daily life where I can in order to help lead by example. In my daily work, I try to be the person with some of the answers and not just be a part of the problem. Over the last five years, I have worked at a fairly high level within the State of Ohio Government in the Information Technology organization. It was my first experience in working at an executive level of an organization. One of the things that struck me is how busy executives are and how little face time you can get with them to present issues and problems. I'm not sure I was always successful but I tried to come in not only with problems but potential solutions as well. In addition, many problems at a high level of the organization are very stressful and I have tried to lead by example and set a positive working attitude working through the problems to help set a positive tone for everyone dealing with the issues. Being positive while working with stressful problems is a lot harder than you might think.

One of the long-term goals I have for myself is to be in a better position to give more back to the community. Over the last few years, I was working a full-time job while teaching in the evenings and on weekends. I am hoping that I can soon reach a balancing point where I have more flexibility in my work to be able to program in some more time to devote to some community programs that I believe can help people in their lives and I have more time to lead by my own examples.

I hope that you too can identify some strong role models in your life that helped you establish your own leadership style. I also hope you have the time and opportunity to use your leadership in a way that is fulfilling and rewarding to yourself and others.

13 Build It Yourself

"You can design and create, and build the most wonderful place in the world. But it takes people to make the dream a reality. "
Walt Disney

I have talked a lot about my Dad in this book, but now it is time to talk about Mom. How could I possibly leave her out? Anyway, in this chapter, I am going to talk about being a bit more self-reliant and what that can mean to you both being able to do things to have a sense of accomplishment as well as the chance to grow as a person.

When I was growing up my father traveled frequently for his job. It became a tradition with my Mom and me to take on some type of project while he was gone and to do something my mother had queued up as a project in her mind. In fact, it became so regular that as soon as he would get home from the airport, be would start looking around the house or yard for the project we did while he was gone. This tradition reached its peak when my mother had decided she wanted a fish pond and fountain in the backyard. She and I had talked about this project for some time. She had a fishpond at her house as a child and always wanted another one. We discussed this at length and talked about ideas of how this could be built. Although we were not poor by any stretch of the imagination, building this pond using contractors would be an expensive proposition. At some point, she just proclaimed to me, "let's just build this ourselves!"

I was in high school at the time and really did not have any construction experience and was trying to imagine in my mind how my mother and I could just go out and build this. My mother can be very persuasive and she eventually talked me into it. I can't remember how long my father was gone, but by the time he was home we had cleared out a huge swath of existing landscaping and build a basic retaining wall, pond, and associated fountain. Several years later a mason followed up after our initial work to help solidify the retaining wall. However, my Mother and I completed all of the original construction. When my father got home he really loved the work and was also greatly relieved that he did not have to be involved. He really hated to do any type of yard work. The pond still stands to this day and is pictured above.

The reason I mention this project, other than being a great family story, is how my mother was able to take me out of my comfort zone and really take on a challenging project. Many times we are faced with situations where we might see some opportunity, but the self-doubt takes over and then we shut down the idea. The doubt becomes so strong that we become risk averse as people. We become so programmed to our daily nine to five world that when we are confronted with new and exciting opportunities we look at them in a very negative way. Maybe my example here is a very simple one and building a small pond and wall in the backyard does not represent a high risk, but my Mom's attitude of building it yourself represents a sense of self-reliance that is sometimes difficult to find in today's world.

Both my mother and father came from a generation where they did not have a great deal of reliance on someone else to go out and make things happen for them. Their attitude in most situations was if you want to do something you needed to just lay out a plan and go and get it done. They fully realized that most of the time it would require hard work and sacrifice to make this happen, but that did not scare them off. This did not mean that they would take on all projects blindly, but they also did not immediately reject a project or task if it meant getting their hands dirty.

With this thought in mind, what are those things in your life that you can build yourself? What are those things you have wanted to do, but the self-doubt is holding you back? Are those things that are holding you back really impediments to you moving forward or have put up roadblocks in your mind? Your mind can be a powerful ally in getting things done, but it can also force you to go down the well-traveled path of least resistance. Not all projects and goals in your life will require you to make some lofty decision to change your life, but learning to push yourself at times can pay great dividends.

I don't visit my Mom as much as I should, but every time I go to her house and walk through the backyard I see the fish pond and think of the time when Mom and I were out there building it. I hope the next time you are faced with some type of opportunity you will consider "building it yourself"!

14 Become You 2.0

"Stay hungry, stay foolish."
Steve Jobs

This chapter was a later addition to this book, but it is certainly not an afterthought. In this chapter, I will describe the journey I went through to change my career from being heavily involved in software development and IT operations to becoming a full-time author and educator.

After working in many different roles in software development and the IT industry, I had reached a stage of burnout where I really needed to find something else. It was not the case with me that I had the usual fits in trials and tribulations with my day job. Instead, I had fundamentally become burned out on the rigors of running large and complex systems. This work often required me to work long hours and fix problems during nights, weekends and holidays.

If you have never worked in an IT operations environment, it can be extremely demanding. I had worked my way up the food chain to become a manager of a large department and had responsibilities for several mission-critical systems that required my constant attention. Many times this work required me to work on nights, weekends and holidays. It had become challenging to escape from work and to have a little bit of quiet time in order to recharge. Through the results of several promotions, I had risen to a reasonably high level within my IT organization. This job had several good perks to go along with it that included a private parking place, a large corner office, and a great staff. If I had looked at it several years earlier in my career, this would have been my dream job. However, once I reached this level, I found that I was fundamentally unhappy with the daily grind and the constant problems with these large systems. It was difficult to explain my unhappiness to my family and friends. They merely saw the perks of my job and not much of the downside.

Toward the end of my software development career, I began teaching in the evenings to make a little extra money and to help pay expenses. Through this experience, I began to find work that was much more gratifying and flexible. Also, at this time, I began to experiment with publishing my own courses online and started writing my first books. After a year or so of this, I began to think about how I might transition out of IT development and pursue a career in education. I also knew that it would be a challenge to replace my current income that I was making in the software development world. Education jobs typically pay very low.

I also knew that I would have to completely reinvent myself and develop new skills for my new role in education. Thankfully I was able to develop the skills on a part-time basis while I was teaching at local universities in the evenings. This experience proved to be invaluable as I began to build my own content and look for a full-time role where I could replace my income for the day job.

It was also vital for me to have a role model that I could look to who had gone through a successful career transformation that I could look to for inspiration. Thankfully one of my good friends, Brent Harder had successfully gone through a career transformation just a few years earlier. Brent and I had worked together for several years on various IT projects. Brent worked for an IT staffing company and worked to help provide contractors on some of the software development projects that I was managing. His role in staffing would often become complicated and fraught with problems. We were managing huge and expensive projects that had tight deadlines. Finding high-quality staff for these types of projects can be extremely challenging. Also, managing the performance of these contractors is an arduous task.

While working with Brent, we became friends and began to discuss our careers and our fundamental dissatisfaction with our current career paths. One of the common interests that we discussed over lunch was that we both had a great interest in exploring the process of investment planning. It was at this time that Brent began to develop a plan to become a full-time stock broker. He also shared the concern that I had about the potential loss of income and the uncertainty of a new career. Ultimately he pulled the trigger and decided to pursue a full-time job as a stockbroker and successfully made the transition over the course of a couple of years. He is now a full-time broker and has risen through the ranks in his company and really enjoys what he does for a living.

Brent and I have remained friends to this day, and I often tell his story to some of my coworkers that are considering a career change. Brent also manages my family's investments and has been a great help in managing and planning my mother finances as well.

With some motivation from my friend Brent and some of the experiences that I had gained teaching part-time, I began to work on my own career transformation and set off on the path for a full-time career in education. I will tell you that this transformation was challenging. I had to convince my wife that this transformation was something worthwhile that I had to do—and it was not just a whim.

I first started my transition by stringing together several part-time teaching rolls at local universities and had put together a small cash reserve to see me through about six months of work. With that in hand, I quit my job and began teaching full time and also used some of the spare time to work on my books and self-publishing video classes. Even with multiple positions, I'd still taken a considerable salary cut and was very nervous about the prospects moving forward.

Along with writing some books, and publishing some courses on Udemy, I had put many videos out on YouTube as part of marketing my books and video courses. I'm not particularly good at marketing, but I have had reasonably substantial success in growing my YouTube channel. I had developed a relatively large base of about a hundred and fifty or so technical videos. During this time, I received an email from someone who worked within an education company, and they had seen my videos. They were wondering if I might be interested in working as a full-time author for them. The company was Linux Academy, and I eventually went on to interview with them and was hired as a full-time course author.

This turned out to be the ideal opportunity for my career change. I have been at Linux Academy for a little over a year it has been a fantastic career experience for me. I now work with like-minded people for a company that produces fabulous training materials. It also has the benefit that the company is in a position to change people's lives in a positive way. Linux Academy is far and above the best company that I've ever worked for.

Although like most people, the fundamental change for me happened on a random break that I had not planned on happening. I feel that this opportunity would not have arisen had I not and experimenting producing content on multiple channels and actively pushing to change my career. Fundamentally changing and reinventing yourself requires you to push the envelope and experiment with new things and take risks. For you to do this, you really have to be inspired and have the self-confidence that you can reach your end goals through hard work and persistence. Good luck on becoming you 2.0!

15 Change the World!

"Education is the most powerful weapon which you can use to change the world."
Nelson Mandela

With some of my parting thoughts in this book, I encourage you to dream on a large scale. When I talk about these types of things I am not talking about a super huge payday or the chance for you to buy a mega yacht. (Although I hope that can happen for you!) I am talking about your opportunity to change the world a little bit at a time over a very long period of time. You can't underestimate how a simple act of kindness or help in someone's life may make a truly profound difference in a community.

Amazon's company mission statement is to be "the world's most customer-centric company." Wow. They did not set out just to be an average retailer and move some product online. They were setting their aim in an unbelievable way. I have done a lot of business with Amazon and they are a truly amazing company. The range of businesses that they are involved in and the worldwide reach of that company is incredible. I don't think it is merely a coincidence that their company slogan reaches for the stars. I'm not saying that simply setting a slogan, or a logo can move you to unbelievable heights, but setting the mindset in yourself and those you interact with can do so.

It's very easy in today's world to let people around you set your own expectations for you.

If you find yourself on the treadmill of life plodding relentlessly through one day after the other, you need to find that spark that will allow you the chance to change the direction in your life. This is extremely difficult to do. If you have entrepreneurial aspirations as I do, many people will think you are crazy.

You should have seen the looks on my family's faces when I told them I was going to teach online and sell video courses. They thought I had truly slipped over the edge. Once I started building a poor man's video studio in the basement they were convinced I had truly lost it. I just kept "chipping away" and moving ahead with my idea. Although I did have a goal to make money online, I also had the idea to share some of my experience with beginning programmers all over the world and offer them the opportunity over the long term to have access to truly world-class software development training. I am still pressing ahead with this and my way to my target audience is through a series of free video classes I have published on YouTube. My goal is to have the world's largest YouTube channel that offers free training for Software developers around the world as well as some of my higher end commercial content. There! I finally said it out loud and on paper. This is my opportunity to change my part of the world.

I'm not saying every goal in your life has to be over the top, but if you have the chance and the right situation, go for it. Go all in! Writing this book is so far out of my comfort zone you can't believe. When I started writing this, I think I had the goal of every author to sell millions of copies and retire to the beach. Although that would be great, at this point I am really hoping that just one idea on one page in this book will help inspire one person into action to help themselves or someone else in their life.

I have published several books to date and the more I write the more I enjoy it. I love the idea of being able to publish to a worldwide audience from my home office. The services available for self-publishing really make the dream of becoming an author more available than it has been in the past. The other day I got a copy of my first book in print. I may never make enough money to write full time online, but holding that book in my hand crossed off a bucket list item in my life. There were many times I almost bailed on my project, but I am really glad I pressed ahead. I would much rather have tried something and failed than not have tried at all.

If you look at most professions, there has to be a first time for everything. For a pilot, it is that first solo flight, for the author it is the first book, for the surgeon it is that very first operation. I could go on and on with the list, but you get the idea. For most of us, that first time is really scary—so scary that most of us will blow it off. I'm sure many people would love to express themselves in a book or article, but that fear of the first time really shuts them down. I remember when I first met my wife she saw me make a presentation at work and commented that I was a natural and wondered how that was so easy for me to do. She had not seen the train wreck presentations that I did when I was first out of college. I'm telling you I had some real first class disasters, but over time I practiced more and more until it became routine. I have the same experience with producing videos for my online classes. So whatever it is that is holding you back, try and get past that first-time blocker—you will be glad you did.

I hope that some of the material in this chapter will help you think of some of those opportunities in your life to set a new direction or embark on a new business or adventure in your life. If the setting is right going big! I think in today's society we idolize people who really hit it big like Bill Gates or Steve Jobs, but we doubt someone that we know can pull off a similar task of greatness. Worse yet, we often put doubts on ourselves.

Colleges and universities do not teach entrepreneurship (OK, maybe a class or two), but rather they prepare us for a career working for someone else. Working a career for someone else is not necessarily a bad thing, but without individuals who are willing to take a chance and put their own spin on things the world would miss out on an incredible amount of innovation.

If you are on the fence, I encourage you to give it a try. Figure out a way to get started. Start small and prove out your idea. Stay up late, get up early, work on your weekend, but give your dream a legitimate shot. Even if you start small, aim high and change the world!

15 Summary

Thank you so much for reading this book. I really hope some of the life lessons in this book have provided some value to you or perhaps some inspiration that can help you get over the hump for your next major project. In addition, I hope this book has uplifted you in some small way and might help you deal with some difficult situations you are working through. Life can be very challenging and can change at a moment's notice. My hope is that from some of the examples in this book, you might be able to make one of your life's situations just a little bit better.

I would like to thank all of the role models I have mentioned in this book. Pastor Tim, please know that I did not sleep through all of your sermons! I have already mentioned my dad numerous times in this book but wanted to add just one more mention of his great love and support to my entire family. I have also mentioned my Mom in this book as well and I just wanted her to know how much I love her and value her continued support. I would like to have a huge shout out and thank you to my mother-in-law Diane for being both a mentor to me but also being my editor as well! Last but not least, thank you to my immediate family, my wife Amy and my daughter Alexandra and my son Eric Jr. who inspire me every day. There are many other people that have inspired me in my life and helped me in so many ways that I can't remember them all, so if I did not mention you it was merely an oversight.

Thank you again and please be sure and leave a review for this book as I would love to hear from you. Good luck on your next adventure!

16 About the Author

Eric Frick

Eric Frick has been involved in software development and information technology operations for 30 years with experience as a Software Developer, Software Development Manager, Software Architect and as an Operations Manager. In recent years he has taught courses in various Computer Science related subjects at a number of universities within the central Ohio region. In 2015 he founded destinlearning.com and is in the process of developing a series of online classes and books that provide practical information for a variety of computer science and software development topics. He currently works as a full time author for Linux Academy. You can view his courses there at https://linuxacademy.com. You can also visit his author page on Amazon for his other publications here: http://bit.ly/erfrick

www.ingramcontent.com/pod-product-compliance
Lightning Source LLC
Chambersburg PA
CBHW052100070526
44584CB00017B/2271